Iris's Wild Ride

Written by Catherine Baker

Illustrated by Elissambura

Collins

She liked to graze in the fields and munch the sweet hay.

Each year, the alpacas had a Sports Day.

When Sports Day started, Iris liked to hide.

You lot make me feel tired!

"Run with us, Iris!" said, Miles.
"You might win a prize!"

But Iris stayed away from the starting line.

The rest of the alpacas began lining up.

Iris sat in the shade. But then she felt a sharp bite!

9

The insect bite felt like fire! Iris jumped, but the insect did not slide off.

Iris did a wild jump. She banged into the tree and ...

... the farm cat landed SPLAT on Iris's back!

Iris sprinted down the field. She jumped across the stile, into the farmer's garden.

The farmer's wet socks and vests were on the line.

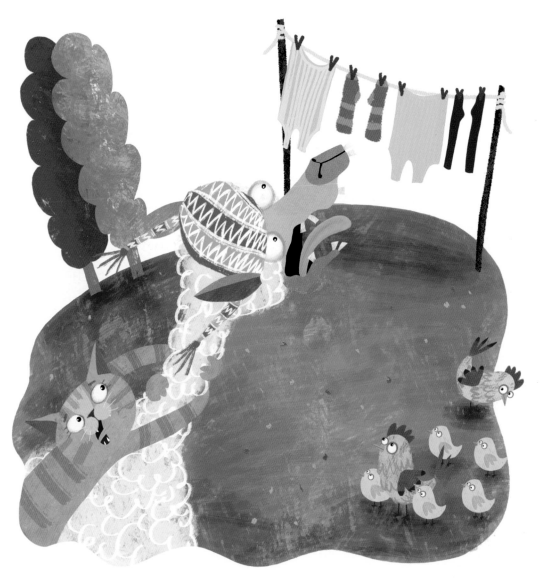

Crash! All the wet items ended up on Iris's neck.

Iris jumped across the gate and started sliding down the lane.

There was LOTS of mud and slime!
Iris and the cat went quicker and quicker.

They went gliding down to the end of the lane. Iris did a jump, back into the field.

Sports Day had just begun.

A wild monster!

19

Iris sprinted down the field, and across the finishing line!

"Iris!" smiled Miles. "You get the prize!"
The cat got a prize too!

Iris's wild ride

22

 Review: After reading

Use your assessment from hearing the children read to choose any GPCs, words or tricky words that need additional practice.

Read 1: Decoding
- Challenge the children to find words in the story with "-ing" and "-ed" endings and to read them aloud:

  -ing (e.g. page 7 *starting*, page 8 *lining*, page 16 *sliding*, page 18 *gliding*, page 20 *finishing*)

  -ed (e.g. page 5 *started, tired*, page 7 *stayed*, page 13 *sprinted*, page 15 *ended*)
- Look together at page 15. Ask the children to find words with the /igh/ sound. (*items, Iris's, like*) Ask them to read them aloud.

Read 2: Prosody
- Choose two double page spreads and model reading with expression to the children. Ask the children to have a go at reading the same pages with expression.
- On pages 11 and 12 show the children how you pause for ellipses to build the suspense.
- Reread the whole book to model fluency and rhythm in the story.

Read 3: Comprehension
- Turn to pages 22 and 23 and ask the children to retell the story in their own words, using the pictures as prompts.
- For every question ask the children how they know the answer. Ask:
  - On pages 4 and 5, why do you think Iris doesn't want to join in with Sports Day? (*she likes to rest and eat hay*)
  - On page 11, why did Iris do a wild jump? (e.g. *to get the insect off her back*)
  - On page 13, did Iris run fast? How do you know? (*Yes, she sprinted down the field*)
  - On page 21, why did the cat get a prize too? (*because it passed the finishing line at the same time as Iris*)
  - Which part of the story did you like the most? Why?